Black Cat

A POETRY COLLECTION

SHIRLEY SIATON

A POETRY COLLECTION

Copyright © 2023 Shirley Siaton-Parabia

ALL RIGHTS RESERVED.
No part of this book may be reproduced or used in any manner without the prior written permission of the copyright owner, except for the use of brief quotations in a book review. To request permission, contact the publisher at books@inkysword.com.

ISBN 978-6-21-837486-7

Published by Shirley S. Parabia
Illustrations by Rein Geronimo
Interior Layout by Mhy San Miguel

First Edition, June 2023

Inky Sword Book Publishing
Barangay Quezon, Arevalo, Iloilo City 5000
Republic of the Philippines
inkysword.com

To Arya
For love of books and black cats

Black Cat
A POETRY COLLECTION

Contents

IX | *Acknowledgments*

Part One: Diffusion
15 | My Death Man
17 | Blue
19 | Dust
21 | Regression
23 | Long-Lost Tango
25 | Solstice
27 | Rainfall
29 | Purple Scrunchie
31 | Faceless
33 | Drought
35 | Yellow-Green
37 | Smoke

Part Two: Negation
43 | Hungry
45 | Silence
47 | Bitten
49 | The Voyage
51 | Begging Streets
53 | Ugly
55 | Wallflower
57 | Fallen Frame

59 | Scars in Solitude
61 | Juxtaposition
63 | Cradled Head
65 | Ulcer
67 | First Taste
69 | Blood
71 | Smoke 2
73 | Pimple

Part Three: Regeneration
79 | Food Court
81 | Lavender Polish
83 | Other
85 | Hidden
87 | Drunk
89 | Lover
91 | A Fat Girl Thing
93 | Flight
95 | Holy War
97 | Back in the Food Court
99 | Black Cat

Acknowledgments

This collection has literally been decades in the making. I never would have had the courage to start writing poems without The Philippine Star *weekend youth section, 'Young Star', the first national publication to shine a spotlight on my poetry.*

To my daughter, Arya, for making me fall in love with books all over again. She read through the entire first draft of this manuscript like a boss, out loud.

Special thanks to Mimi—publishing coordinator, legal advisor and, above all, mother.

Finally, to my husband, Peter, who provided unwavering support as I embarked on the journey of getting my books out into the world. I could never have asked for a better person to share my life with, now and always.

> "..striking bolt, tearing
> apart into vestiges of what
> I was once…"

One day, straight after winning a national journalism competition, I put a piece of paper into my trusty portable typewriter and started writing 'Passengers,' a poem inspired by the fleeting nature of life, the things we leave behind, and the movie 'The Crow II: City of Angels.' The rest, as they say, is history.

Before my poetry saw publication in a national periodical, no one really believed I was capable of writing in this genre.

The pieces in this chapter constitute my earliest work. These are random poems inspired by things and events both captivating and mundane. This is the time when the words and verses left my headspace, fearlessly diffusing ideas into the greater, wider world.

my death man

..with thinning breath...

lightning strikes you
and you stand ramrod
straight
silver bullets pounce
on your obsidian heart
and you stand
impervious

what's your name,
my death man?
who are you
to take my breath
away
and leave me
seeking?
my death man,
come to me
relieve me of misery

SHIRLEY SIATON

the acid shower
caresses
your unyielding face
that I yearn to caress—
the downpour is reduced
to the trickles
of music
from your splintered guitar

daggers of desolation
draw your black-red blood
and my lips savor
its metal tang
then I drink
of your madness
and the coldness
of your love

my death man,
your music is my eternal lullaby
my death man,
your music is my elegy

blue

..the spectrum's dull edge...

Ending in a shattered
pot of clay:
no gold, yet the arch
(seven-tiered)
pours its sorrows
to overflowing.

Pattering on the
stained-glass edifice
of Saints, their halos
threatening to break
from the strain
of false reverence—
the shower
from heaven disbelieved.

Prisms falling
to cut against
cracked skin
with untrue tales
to tell.

When the gray tormented
shall clear away
doubtful Time alone knows;
the blue canvas, white-dotted,
my blinded eyes may
never behold.

dust

..swirling to form what we pick ...

Drowning scratchy tones
screeched by a podium voice
that remains ever faceless:
subdued, a clacking staccato.

Rock-encrusted earth, weeded not for years,
chipped away in vain
by the dull-edged shovel;
crooked steel churning
visions acres wide.

In the purplish twilight glow
sparse through the sun-browned canopies,
a hunched soul
squints
as if grasping lost fragments
from hazy-gray auto exhausts.

Close to the lone theater's
cobbled threshold—
bidding two-bit thespians
(so-called)
Welcome.

Once the dustman;
a shrine of wrath and glory
long since crumbled
to bits.

He pounds
against the unrelenting soil
'til dusk
cloaks
a sleepy world.

regression

..homesick in the storm...

Diverging paths
leading to somewhere
nowhere and everywhere
mud
and quashed
to rain-wet mush.

Singing voice
breaking through
falling and drenching
straggler
and lost
in the vat of destiny.

Striking bolt
tearing apart
into vestiges of what I was
once
and homeward
I plod on.

long-lost tango

...the mime's perfected footwork...

How Time went past
driving ever southward
like sunbeams
welcoming dusk.

Songs long forgotten
lose what little melody
floating about in dreams—
too worn
from a quest
of finding fragments
once belonging
to you and me.

As the unknown dawns
once more: if we could dance
and know no fear
to the beat
of the long-lost tango.

Even if
scratchy phonographs
play silent music alone.

solstice

..when seasons dissipate into the madness...

the voice
of a Jack or Jill
echoes
like a song from elementary school
"bah bah black sheep..."
haunting
taunting

"have you any wool?"
none, except what's pulled
over my eyes
with their long standing myopia;
if only the wool
could double as a coat
to ward off
the chill of uncertainty

then again,
the (El Nino) heat
radiates
from my tuffet of safety
where to go
where to go (?)
I no longer know

the spider
I await
to keep me company

"twinkle, twinkle little star…"
things, I no longer wonder
what they are
all are just specks
of dust
in my high-powered vacuum cleaner

a solstice
of worlds that made me
now knitted
like frayed maroon yarn
of a friendship bracelet
I had worn through

a keepsake
enduring
as seasons
come and go

rainfall

..allegory of liquid fire...

Witches' brew
    enthralling stray spirits
    that dare to savor
    its citrus lure
Sumptuous
A prison of unseen walls.

Blessed water
    soothing the sting of emptiness
    that eats away
    my life
Cool
An omen of redemption.

Fluid veil
    deceiving eyes that pry,
    that seek to see
    my unilinear teardrops
Translucent
As the salty stream.

SHIRLEY SIATON

Acid wine
    scorching like lust
    that drunken poets fancy
    in many a sonnet
Intoxicating
A being stripped of dreams.

purple scrunchie

..beyond its elasticity...

The first time
I used the five-peso
terry elastic
was on a humid
November day.
It should have been
chilly,
but no.
It was humid.

And singing rain
yet to spill
its costly droplets
on cracked brains
and unused recycled-paper notebooks
strewn haphazardly
throughout school.

To capture tendrils
of a bad-hair day
(yet again)
that sweep the particulates
from bitter-tasting
air:
the scrunchie left
my pulse
and took its beat away.

faceless

..a couch potato's love...

Images of you
flicker
as candle-flames do
in a sultry night.

(Beckoning.)

Your voice
ripples
as molten gold does
in the North Wind's fleeting embrace.

I curse
the wrinkled paper
on which I draw
the eyes that had never laid on me.
I hate
the leaky pen
that sputters an endearment
or two
you may never even hear.

I wish
you were the remote control
I hold close
until sign-off.
That way,
there would be no more
goodbye.

drought
..in pain, and seeking...

Yesterday
there was rain
in torrents
tearing away what is
and in hesitant streams
trickling as tears would.

Now
dried
and fraught with madness
rain is no more
and long gone.
Puddles pool
as final remembrance
slipping away
in the midday
heat.

yellow-green
..waiting for the fall...

I see the golden rays
    glimmer
against my squinting eyes
against the Crocs-clad feet
that wear the pavement thin.

When, walking by,
with olive flesh
and a hundred hopes
and the murmur of second chances—

You look through my
sun-curtained visage
like it isn't there
scribbling dreams away
    crookedly
picking the dried grass
    to bits.

When you're now
    the past
the fallen swipe of life:
you are the veined leaf
    fluttering
in the summer wind.

smoke

..carcinogenic lust...

His name
is a word I could
not pronounce
nor spell.

All I do
is roll it around
my nicotine-stained
tongue
but never
say it or exhale
it like smoke.

Like, your being
kills me
with every breath.

negation

> "..the void: where my tongue-tips
> catch the essence
> of a hungering moon…"

In quite a few fields of study, the act of 'negation' is often perceived as doing something destructive or detrimental.

As someone who loved Algebra (thanks to Emellie Palomo, may she rest in power), I have personally regarded the concept as doing the inverse, flipping something the other way, and, of course, creating a new outcome so disparate from the original.

It was time to challenge the norm.

It was time for people to hear a different voice, to see through a different pair of eyes.

I attempted to capture simple concepts and make them intricate and fascinating. The poems in this chapter are perhaps my most subversive, uninhibited and ornate ones.

hungry
..for you...

The sustenance has gone stale,
and I don't want to swallow
perforated hopes that ride
the stillness and the emptiness
as I gaze at you.

Maybe you remind me
that I want to put something
in the void that throbs to be filled
so it can live-
and I think
I no longer want to.

I try so hard
to go down the pipes
like dishwater
when I want to drink you in
as my breath:
I still need to.

silence

..nothing but love's death...

living under the tearstained sky
left all alone and staring
way up high
at the gray
or whatever color in my way

I saw nothing
but the blinding dusk
I felt nothing but your touch
burning my life away
in memory you killed me

with one look
nothing matters but the pain
that I want from your caress
and you never say a word
to make me
catch my breath again

go away to the songs that you sing
to the crash of glass
as the shrapnel cuts into you
I hope you bleed
I hope your life spills
like the milk
that I cry over

Bitten

..healing from red welts...

I've been scratched and stabbed,
wounded to the point
of losing blood.
But I've never been hurt
the way I had
when I was bitten
by the bug.

Bitten now and bleeding:
there's nothing in those sterile shelves
to ease my pain;
I just need you
not to pour salt
into my gaping heart.

the voyage

..on growing up as me...

Cutting through waves,
a swath of foam;
green-gray curdles
trail underfoot.

The raft of makeshift hopes
adrift for days-
and aimless-
steered blindly on.

Beyond the mist,
cobbles and rock-bits
make an inexorable testament
to lands beyond.

begging streets
..a postcard's negative...

Faceless, they contort
and silently scream
paper dolls
hanging on the clothesline
slapped
slapped about
by starched-white shirts
in virginal mockery.

A coin-regurgitated gumball:
cherry, chewed
staining
the betelnut-stained
pearly whites
flashed to starving
manual cameras running promises
ran dry.

SHIRLEY SIATON

                Fluffy-gray air bubbles
                from oily fire hydrants
                        give
                  the cleansing rain
                  in a summer spell,
                  as darker streams
            wear down the asphalt gutter:
                  hence, not potable.

                   Falling, and struck
                        the can
                       wrenched
                 to its wounding gape;
                        inside,
                  the doughnut-like
                     copper coin
                        hears
                the slightest plaintive cry
                      of thanks.

ugly

..in and out...

a visage ripples crookedly

watch, as the looking glass
peels what is reflected
away

leaving a heart
never known to beat
in pulses
but in dreams left unrealized
to fester, unseen
to wilt away
in disconsolate bits of brown,
unremembered

SHIRLEY SIATON

---

       thus, comes the time
   to walk the thin dividing line
    between you and yourself
       and see nothing
through the endless masquerade

       (you hate it-
         much)

wallflower

..rearranging my heart...

Bitterness embeds
itself
deep down.

And
I find myself
wishing
to see black-red
blood
stain your purity,
your hypocrisy.

You suck.

fallen frame

..broken...

It's time to shut the door
and close it all away.
Since I've lost
what there is
to cry for.

It's time to put the razor blade
back on the shelf
(carefully, as not to nick
the fingertips with which I write)
and be like a clam:
tightly closed up.

Pry open with the tines,
if you dare,
when no one can.
No one can look
into this little world
and not be blinded.

SHIRLEY SIATON

It's time to pick up
the bits
of the picture frame
that found its way
off the peg.
But the photo's
left unscathed.

It's time to gather
the strewn odes
and flush them down the drain
and shout a slurred
"Nevermore!"
to an unheeding world.

As the fallen frame pieces,
thrown bit by bit
out of the window,
cut into hands
that had brushed away
silent salty rivers.

scars in solitude

..as they are free...

Child, let your pain speak
let the scar fade
after the crucible
of silent shackles.

Leaves, aphid-white
drift there- and away;
a hope in balmy
rooms of soot.

Framed lovingly:
twisted images
of lost dreams
grasped in passing.

juxtaposition

..severed from a dream...

Soar high
in unbounded flight,
tread new-mown blades
with reverence.

'Tis the temple
of olden faith
borne witness
to glory and bloodshed.

With armaments splintered,
was carted away
to watch- and weep-
on the cruel stone stage.

cradled head

..a eulogy of sorts...

Now I try to say
sorry
and there's this stopper
up my larynx.
Unspoken remains
my regret.

There is the first
bitter whiff of bloom
thrown into the welcoming cradle;
the first gentle stab
into my weakling's fingers-
that thorn's vengeance.

I felt the ire
in its half-wilted petals.
Felt the blood
dry a deep red;
the pain a dull
thrumming in waxy ears.
Nothing more
but wind, smells,
and gooseflesh.

Longing for that resented
touch on my migraine-inhabited
head.
The throbbing flesh mixes
with the dewy earth.

ulcer

..recurring lament...

Would you end
the stabbing pain-?
Planted, plunged
deep into my gut:
a knife
that nothing wielded
no one held
but you.

first taste

..acquaintance night...

Pounding.

The weary floor resonates:
infectious with life and sound,
with strobes of varicolored light.
In flashes.
As fast as the young heart
pumps life,
as sharp as the senses
take in the reek of body heat.

My bareness
is shaped by your hands;
I move to the rhythm
shared by lone strangers
amidst the frenzy.
I forget the bitch wind
of night.

This is but the first touch.

As the swirling
gathers me into its billows,
I hold on to flesh, bone,
the unmasked scent of soap
and the unmistakable froth of anger
bubbling from burnished lips
and distinctly hear

The pounding.

blood

..breathing life...

Thank you.
For the pain
through which I grope my way
in dazed wakefulness.
The void, where
my tongue-tips
catch the essence
of a hungering moon.

Thank you.
For the mead-like meat
of thoughts
long struck by paradox.
Scratching away.
Clawing, until the coagulating life
ensues to stream.
Wanderlust, and more.

Thank you.
For the flesh,
bathed in endless moaning
trembles.
Lined with pain
from endless moaning
trembles.
For the flesh,
seeking the uneven
tease.

Thank you.
For the constancy.
The mundane.
This strange little
taste that leaves
a parched throat half-open.
In expectation.

smoke 2

..my second wind...

I take a toke
of your purity
and realize
the sweetness
exploding within me.

Injecting life
like the amphetamine
in my morning espresso
or the cheap instant
or whatever
coffee in my cup.

The scent filling
my being—
that heady scent
is your frankincense
kiss.

pimple

..when will the alpha-hydroxy kick in..?

Just like a pimple:
You throbbed in my waking hours
taking time
as I tried
to scratch at you.

Just like a pimple:
You grew on me
and swelled—
a sensation
I can no longer
ignore.

I tried to prick you away
but you left me
gaping
and in pain.
Just like a pimple.

regeneration

*"..but then: I always seek,
and find, and feel…"*

Certain creatures are imbued with the ability to grow lost limbs again. Human beings are in possession of a far more superior gift: The capacity to hope, even in the face of great adversity.

The poems in this book's final chapter aim to capture the indefatigable hope in the human spirit, the very thing that fuels faith, ambition and determination.

I have seen hope thrive in the darkest, most decrepit of places. I have witnessed remarkable stories of resilience and survival, pain morphing into impenetrable armor, and loss bringing forth new beginnings.

I have learned that true strength is not in holding on, but in letting go.

When the time comes, something greater will grow in its place.

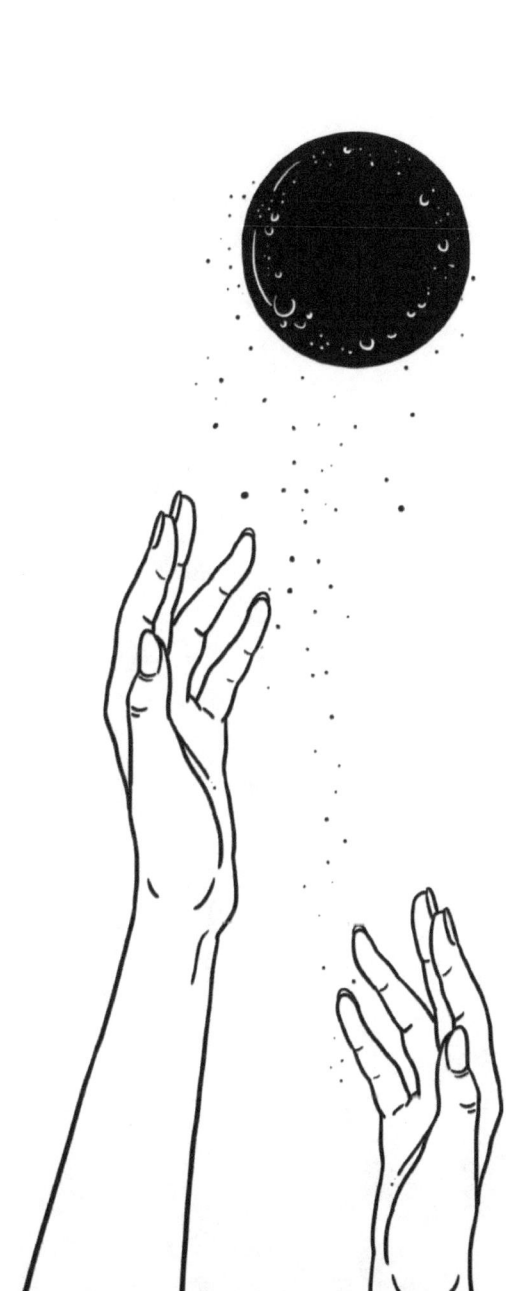

food court

..break time...

He sits
on the mocha-brown wood
and watches
the angst-ridden crowd
sweep by
like the dust
he used to sweep
when the back
still held.

(There is no end to them.)

He stays
unperturbed
in their midst
and hungers
for what he now cooks
(squid balls)
but can no longer afford
to sink
his (long gone) teeth
into.

He counts
in silent vigil
the cruel notes
of the cacophony
overwhelming
his time-ravaged senses.

He waits
for the minutes
of his half-hour work break
to pass
the way he waits
for the throng
to leave him
in its dusty wake.

lavender polish

..a little self-care...

i. drizzles of laundry water
strip the shade
I had blended
from fleeting dreams;
leaving bare unlovely,
uneven surfaces
no one would look at
(not even me)

ii. I scrub
the roughness
with a cotton ball
drenched in fortified-protein
hopes,
and I cringe;
the lavender fades
as would the bruises
from a post-Happy Hour
tantrum
he had thrown
countless times before:

SHIRLEY SIATON

---

iii. now, I shake
 the bottle
 vigorously
 just so I could
 paint the frosted purplish hue
 on my nails
 to color-coordinate

iv. I wait
 for the lavender
 to set
 to reappear
 on my flesh

other

..graduation day...

I was the one
Who looked at you from way across the room
The one who felt your pain
And never gave it back
I cared not
If you can't even see
Just in dreams
Be with me

I was the girl
Who felt your touch
On her flesh
That gentleness from someone so strong
I cried not
If you love her
Just go on
Walking past

SHIRLEY SIATON

I was the other
You looked right through
I was part of you
That shudder in the hall
That whisper into the moonless sky
That gaze on your back as you walk towards her
That one
Loving you

hidden

..bracing for impact...

I never knew you,
I never even looked at you—
but there you were
a shadow among shadows.
If only I took the time
to see.

I heard you then:
a loud drumbeat after the next,
pounding to the steady rhythm
of a heart
long since watching
and waiting.

Now, I watch the unyielding downpour
wash away time
in runny puddles.
Now, I listen to the clock
ticking away,
taunting.

And I wait
for the moment—
that killing blow
when you turn
and walk away.

drunk

..too much of a good thing...

Spun me around
in circles;
I took much
out of nothing
that was already there.

An emptiness
once filled to the brim
with everything
that mattered.

A wholeness
I swore
would never break.

Then again,
you came
and shattered it all
and made me
seek what I am.

lover

..a megane complex...

When do you look?

There's nothing more
to life
but net and lines.

Of service overs and smashes;
squeaking and worn rubber shoes
against the cold concrete court
against the dreamscape.

This is a game of you, for you.

Forgetting and remembering
in glances
as fast as you move.

There is blood
beneath the sweat.

When do you see?

a fat girl thing

..a treatise on exploration...

hanging over
a hunk of ham, of flesh
a slice of the delicatessen
in my fever dreams

slices, and chunks
ripples of sinfully sweet
saccharine and corn
dripping and my senses
peak
(unbearably)

I but pinch my sides
bruised by the too-tight denims
that cut between the cheeks of my
meandering butt

it always hurts like hell
again, and again

SHIRLEY SIATON

as I look at the emaciated
hoochie mamas
with their belly-tanks,
their platform shoes that do not crack
from the burden,
the silver crosses caressing their
firm (upright) bosoms

my hands find the draping tips
hanging over a rolling middle
to squeeze, and squeeze

flight

..getting domestic...

It's just like a rocket.
I arrive to the careen
of ceramics, an artful juggling
with an unfeeling wall.
And dodge.

The new haircut
left unnoticed, now adorned
with glass bits from jalousies,
beer mugs that always reek,
and glasses that leave stains
on woodwork.

It's just like a home-run hit.
I enter to the incoming rush
of a thirty-peso spatula
and deftly make the catch.

SHIRLEY SIATON

The uniform, rust-stained,
had eaten heartily ahead.
Splotches of tonight's
savory viand, plus the neighbor's
complimentary birthday leche flan.

Thus, I contemplate
a career in sports.

holy war

..another Sunday morning...

i. reckoning
    has come
    my mama tells me
    that I am a heretic
    that I'd rather wear
    my unwashed denim cut-offs
    than kiss the feet
    of elevated saints

ii. Sunday morn
    is a struggle
    when I'd rather keep my eyes
    closed
    and chat to a campy dream-
    conscription
    lamenting
    in Freudian skerries
    than dress in white
    stained twice too many
    by unexpected flows
    'neath the pulpit

iii. a ratty blanket
     too dirty to be washed
     is a shield
     of futility against salvation
     (it ain't free, no)
     that sells itself
     by stealing slumber and cuckoo
     projections
     and Chinese soap operas
     right before teen show reruns

iv. endlessly
     I search for weapons
     but there is no fighting
     a blast
     of the cold shower
     or the threat of cutting off my
     fiat sustenance

v.   the beads I gather

vi. and I head for the final stop
     glossed lips moving
     in silent feverish whispers
     of supplication

back in the food court

..time happens...

The primary-hued neon tubes
make a lurid flashing cacophony—
silently beckoning.
As throngs of weary hearts file by
too careworn to care, or
surreptitiously glance.

In cold mechanical precision
roams the legion
of tightly-clothed brawny
busboys:
Taking the unwanted away,
those abandoned
garish-orange trays.

In this room
where the air is tepid,
and spruced
with the distant memory
of onions
and soda gone flat—
there echo
footfalls of tales unbounded
by number.

But all
just come to pass
in that stream.

black cat

..baptism of fire...

Sign of the cross.

It's a phase like everybody else's:
A bit of futile struggles here (I annotate),
sneezy tears there.
Desire is a lollipop I lick at
and spit its taste away.
Only to visit confession
by cutting class.

Don't forget
the dawn rendezvous
of hazy brown-and-white cylindrical pilings
caressing my breath,
of bitter foam kissing
my burning lips,
of heat cascading
down my neck and throat
and chest
and belly.

The water runs over me, to waken.

But then, I always seek
and find
and feel.

About the Author

Shirley Siaton writes edgy and evocative stories and poems. Her worlds are in a deliciously dark cross-section of the romance, neo-noir, action, fantasy, new adult and contemporary genres.

She has several books of fiction and poetry released since February 2023. Her first book is the free verse collection *Black Cat and other poems.* She also pens juvenile literature as Shirley Parabia.

She is an award-winning writer, poet and journalist in English, Filipino and Hiligaynon, lauded by the Stevan Javellana Foundation, Philippine Information Agency and West Visayas State University. Her essays, short stories and poems have been published internationally in print and digital media. Her multi-lingual plays have been staged in the Philippines.

Shirley is a black belt in Shotokan Karate and an international certified fitness coach. Originally from Iloilo City, she is based in the Middle East with her husband and two daughters.

Links

Shirley's official website:
shirleysiaton.com

Complete reading guide:
shirley.pub

Subscribe to Shirley's VIP list for free exclusive updates:
newsletter.shirleysiaton.com

www.ingramcontent.com/pod-product-compliance
Lightning Source LLC
LaVergne TN
LVHW040107080526
838202LV00045B/3807